W9-BQT-919

FIESTA!
THE FESTIVALS OF MEXICO

Festival decorations hang in a doorway in a Mexican town. The people of Mexico carefully plan and prepare for the rituals of various festivals, since the celebrations are a significant and meaningful part of Mexican culture.

MEXICO
Leading the Southern Hemisphere

FIESTA!
THE FESTIVALS OF MEXICO

MC MASON CREST PHILADELPHIA

Mason Crest
450 Parkway Drive, Suite D
Broomall, PA 19008
www.masoncrest.com

Printed and bound in the United States of America.

CPSIA Compliance Information: Batch #M2014.
For further information, contact Mason Crest at 1-866-MCP-Book.

First printing
1 3 5 7 9 8 6 4 2

Library of Congress Cataloging-in-Publication Data
       on file at the Library of Congress

        ISBN: 978-1-4222-3217-0 (hc)
        ISBN: 978-1-4222-8682-1 (ebook)

Mexico: Leading the Southern Hemisphere series ISBN: 978-1-4222-3213-2

TABLE OF CONTENTS

MEXICO

Leading the Southern Hemisphere

KEY ICONS TO LOOK FOR:

 Text-dependent questions: These questions send the reader back to the text for more careful attention to the evidence presented there.

 Words to understand: These words with their easy-to-understand definitions will increase the reader's understanding of the text, while building vocabulary skills.

 Series glossary of key terms: This back-of-the book glossary contains terminology used throughout this series. Words found here increase the reader's ability to read and comprehend higher-level books and articles in this field.

 Research projects: Readers are pointed toward areas of further inquiry connected to each chapter. Suggestions are provided for projects that encourage deeper research and analysis.

 Sidebars: This boxed material within the main text allows readers to build knowledge, gain insights, explore possibilities, and broaden their perspectives by weaving together additional information to provide realistic and holistic perspectives.

Chronology of major mexican festivals

Enero (January)
Month dedicated to the Holy Name of Jesus
1 New Year's Day; Solemnity of the Virgin Mary
   2nd Sunday in January, Baptism of the Lord
6 Three Kings Day
17 St. Anthony's Day for the Blessing of the Animals
18 Santa Prisca, Patron Saint of Taxco
20 St. Sebastian the Martyr

Febrero (February)
2 Candlemas
5 Constitution Day
12-14 Ajijic, Jalisco, Mexican National Chili Cook-off Championship
16-18 Xochimilco, D.F., Amaranth Festival
14 Valentine's Day
23-26 Canelas, Durango, Coffee and Guava Fair
24 Flag Day

Marzo (March) Month dedicated to the worship of Saint Joseph
8 St. John of God
11 Dzula, Quintana Roo, Traditional Mayan Food Fiesta
17 St. Patrick, Patron Saint of San Patricio Melaque
18 Nationalization of Petroleum Industry
19 St. Joseph's Day
21 Benito Juárez's Birth; spring equinox

Abril (April)
15-30 Aguascalientes Wine Festival
25 San Marcos, Patron Saint of Aguascalientes

29-30 Tlaxcalancingo, Puebla, Nopal Festival
   30 Children's Day

Mayo (May) Month of flowers consecrated to the Holy Virgin Mary

   1 Labor Day; St. Joseph's Day
1-10 Rosario, Sinaloa, Regional Fruit, Vegetable and Salsa Festival
   3 Holy Cross Day
   5 Battle of Puebla, otherwise known as Cinco de Mayo
  10 Mothers Day
  15 St. Isador the Farmer, Blessing of Animals
15-31 Escárcega, Campeche, Rice Festival
20-28 Tequisquiapan, Querétaro, National Wine and Cheese Fair
22-30 Loma Bonita, Oaxaca, and Pineapple Festival

Other spring holidays whose dates vary from year to year include:
- Carnival
- Shrove (Fat) Tuesday
- Good Friday
- Easter

Junio (June) Month dedicated to the worship of the Sacred Heart of Jesus

   3 Corpus Christi
   4 Pentecost
  13 St. Anthony of Padua
  18 Papantla, Veracruz, Vanilla Festival
     3rd Sunday in June, Father's Day
  24 St. John the Baptist
  27 Our Lady of Perpetual Succor
  29 St. Peter & St. Paul

Julio (July) Month of the Precious Blood of Christ

   4 Our Lady of Refuge
  16 Our Lady of Mount Carmel
17-23 Oaxaca Mescal Festival
18-25 Lunes del Cerro Festival, Oaxaca
  25 St. James the Apostle

Agosto (August)
  3 Ensenada, Baja California, Wine Grape Harvest Festival
  15 The Assumption of the Virgin Mary; Tala, Nayarit, Corn Festival
  20 Gómez Palacio, Durango, Cotton and Grape Fair (runs through Sept. 15)
  28 St. Augustine, Patron Saint of Puebla

Septiembre (September) Month of National Festivities
  1 President's State of the Union Address
  13 Young Heroes of Chapultepec
  14 Horseman's Day
14-16 Surutato, Sinaloa, Peach Fair
  15 Independence Cry
  16 Independence Day
  24 Our Lady of Mercy
  29 St. Michael the Archangel, Patron Saint of San Miguel Allende

Octubre (October) Month dedicated to the Holy Rosary
1-12 Cuetzalán, Puebla, Coffee Fair
1-21 San Pedro Actópan, State of Mexico, Molé Festival
  4 San Francisco de Asís, Patron Saint of Chapala
  7 Our Lady of the Rosary
  12 Columbus Day; Day of the Races; Pilgrimage Guadalajara-Zapopan
14-17 Cholula, Puebla, Bread Fair.

Noviembre (November)
1-2 Day of the Dead
1-14 Chignahuapán, Puebla, Christmas Bread Fair
  2 Day of the Dead; All Souls Day
  12 Mailman's Day
  20 Revolution Day

22 St. Cecilia, Patron Saint of Musicians
28 Gómez Farías, Tamaulipas, Corn Fair (runs through Dec. 28)
30 St. Andrew, Patron Saint of Ajijic

Diciembre (December)
Month of the Nativity of the Lord and of the Virgin of Guadalupe
    6 St. Nicholas
    8 The Immaculate Conception
  12 Nuestra Señora de Guadalupe (Our Lady of Guadalupe)
16-24 Pre-Christmas festivities
  18 Virgin of Soledad Festival, for the patron of Oaxaca
  23 Oaxaca, Radish Festival
  24 Christmas Eve
  25 Christmas Day
  28 Day of the Holy Innocents
  31 New Year's Eve

A colorful float in an Independence Day parade in Mexico City.

 WORDS TO UNDERSTAND

conquistadors—Spanish conquerors of the New World.
piñatas—Brightly colored, papier-mâché shapes containing candy and
small toys.

Mexican girls, accompanied by their chaperone, march in a Cinco de Mayo parade. This festival, held on the fifth of May, is one of the most joyful and widely celebrated of the year.

FIVE THOUSAND FIESTAS
A PARTY EVERY DAY

Accrding to the Mexican Department of Tourism, between 5,000 and 6,000 recognized fiestas (holiday celebrations) are celebrated in Mexico every year. These celebrations are religious, national, local, personal, and food related. On any given day of the year in Mexico, at least one fiesta is being celebrated somewhere in the nation.

Fiestas keep alive the traditions of various individual towns, cities, and states within Mexico. Fiestas also commemorate the important historical anniversaries of the United Mexican States. They pay homage to the special foods and crops of the nation, and they are held for birthdays, baptisms, weddings, and graduations. Some fiestas are thrown to welcome special guests to a town or to a private residence. Mexican postal workers even have their very own fiesta day!

Almost every fiesta in Mexico features special food, music, dancing, arts and crafts, parades, fireworks, parties, and prayer. Some of these celebrations have their own brightly colored costumes. Fiestas may be held in churches, town centers, private clubs, or personal homes.

Oftentimes, though, fiestas are held in the village plaza. Plazas are parks that are generally found in the center of a Mexican city, village, or town. Some plazas are paved with flagstones and lined with benches. Most are filled with beautiful flowers and lovely shade trees.

Piñatas are often hung from the plaza trees during fiestas. The village children take turns trying to break open these bright, candy-filled papier-mâché sculptures. When the piñatas break, the children scramble quickly to gather up as many goodies as they can.

On October 12, Mexicans celebrate the Day of the Races. This day honors all the ethnic groups that have united to form the proud population of Mexico. Mexicans who are a mixture of Indian and Spanish blood are referred to as *mestizos*. *Criollo* is the Mexican name given to Europeans, Americans, and Canadians living in Mexico. *Mulattos* are a mixture of African slaves, who were brought over to Mexico in the 17th and 18th centuries, with Native Americans or mestizos. Native Mexicans are the direct descendants of the Aztecs, Maya, Olmecs, and other indigenous peoples of Mexico.

Mexicans celebrate the major Catholic holy days of Christmas, Easter, and All Saint's Day. Christmas is celebrated differently in Mexico than it is in the United States, however. Mexicans observe the birth of Jesus on December 25, but exchange gifts with friends and family on January 6, or the Day of the Wise Men.

According to Catholic tradition, every day of the year is dedicated to a different saint. These are the days that each saint receives special honor and recognition from Catholics around the world. When the Spaniards came to Mexico during the 16th century, they brought with them the practice of celebrating a person's saint's day. Today, the individual saint's days are as important as birthdays in most Mexican homes. Each individual is honored and

Mexicans wear brilliant, colorful traditional clothing for many celebrations. Fiesta dress for women often includes exotic ornamental hairpieces and flowing skirts, while men wear embroidered vests, pants, and sombreros.

15

celebrated along with his or her saint.

People in Mexico love to celebrate fiestas. Entire villages get together to parade, party, and dance. The entire village or town often seems like one big happy family.

Some historians speculate that the reason Mexicans have so many fiestas is because they need to constantly cheer themselves up. Mexico's history is filled with hardship—conquering invaders, revolutions, poverty, and political turmoil. Mexicans may have a "live for today, for who knows what tomorrow may bring" attitude.

But another, more positive explanation for the number of Mexican fiestas is that these celebrations are simply displays of Mexicans' fierce patriotism. The people of this nation feel intense pride in their past, their religion, and their complex ethnic background. For instance, Mexico has a nationwide celebration called the Day of the Races that celebrates ethnic diversity. Another fiesta day, Cinco de Mayo, celebrates the victory of the Mexican army over the French army

16

Decorative masks line a table at a Mexican market. Mexicans often express themselves through folk art that is created for fiestas and festivals.

at the battle of Puebla on May 5, 1862.

When the Spanish *conquistadors* landed in what is now Mexico, they encountered natives practicing a ritual called the Day of the Dead. In an attempt to Christianize this ritual, the Spaniards moved the fiesta from the ninth month of the Aztec calendar, usually the month of August, to coincided with the Catholic holy days of All Saints' Day and All Souls' Day (November 1 and 2).

The Day of the Races, Cinco de Mayo, and the Day of the Dead are all examples of the different kinds of fiestas celebrated by Mexicans. Fiestas are a means for Mexican families to honor their ancestors and share their memories and traditions with their children. Fiestas are an important joyous element of Mexico's colorful culture.

TEXT-DEPENDENT QUESTIONS

What are three major Roman Catholic holy days that are widely observed in Mexico?

What is celebrated on the Day of the Races (Día de la Raza)?

RESEARCH PROJECT

Cinco de Mayo celebrates a victory by the Mexican army over a French force at the battle of Puebla on May 5, 1862. Learn about the battle, and write a report explaining why the French army was in Mexico, why the French lost the battle, and what the ultimate consequence of the Mexican victory was.

 ## WORDS TO UNDERSTAND

Lent—the 40-day period from Ash Wednesday to Easter.
Mariachi—a form of Mexican music played by street bands.
serenade—to sing outdoors at night, often to a woman.

Mexican soldiers salute during an Independence Day parade on Avenue Reforma in Mexico City. Mexico declared its independence from Spain on September 16, 1810, but the struggle for freedom did not end until 1821.

MEXICO'S NATIONAL HOLIDAYS
VIVA MÉXICO!

The government of Mexico recognizes a select group of national holidays by giving all Mexicans these days off from work. Schools are closed, and the post office, banks, and many other businesses close as well.

January 1 is the fiesta of El Año Nuevo, or New Year's Day. On El Año Nuevo, newly elected officials usually take office. The swearing-in ceremonies are often part of the fiestas. This holiday coincides with the Catholic observance of the Solemnity of the Virgin Mary.

February 5 is Mexico's Constitution Day. Mexico has had six constitutions during its history. The constitutions of 1857 and 1917 were each passed on February 5. The holiday celebrations on this day are marked by official speeches across the nation.

Flag Day is February 24 in Mexico. February 24, 1821, was the date Mexico's War of Independence officially ended and independence was proclaimed. Mexico has celebrated Flag Day every year since 1937. On Flag Day, the people hold great celebrations in front of the memorial statute of General Vicente Guerrero, the first Mexican soldier to swear allegiance to the flag.

March 5 kicks off Carnaval, an official Mexican holiday that consists of a five-day celebration before *Lent*. Beginning on the weekend before Lent, Carnaval is a time for parades, floats, costumes, music, dancing, drinking, and eating. Many people wear costumes and masks, while they dance and walk in parades.

In the evenings during Carnaval fireworks are set off using a traditional *castillo*, or castle (a large fireworks stage). Saturday evening during Carnaval, Mexicans enjoy the coronation of the Carnaval Queen and the silly Ugly King. The *Quema de Mal Humor*, or the burning of bad humor, sets fire to a dummy made to look like some unpopular character.

On Sunday, the biggest parades and fireworks are held. The people dance in the streets. Parents and children stay out together until late in the evening.

Monday brings the Day of the Oppressed Husband. Husbands are allowed to do anything they want, as long as it is legal and moral. They are given 23.5 hours of freedom on this day.

Finally, Fat Tuesday arrives. The people enjoy one last feast while they prepare to go back to

General Ignacio Zaragoza and the Mexican army beat the French in the battle of Puebla on May 5, 1862, even though the French were better equipped and had a much larger army. This battle took place after Emperor Napoléon III of France ordered French troops to conquer Mexico.

After the battle of Puebla, the French gained control of Mexico City. Napoléon established a French-backed government there. In 1866 and 1867, France withdrew its troops from Mexico because of opposition from many Mexicans and the insistence of the United States government.

Before the season of Lent, Mexicans celebrate with a festival called Carnival. Here, people listen to music and dance while riding in colorful canal boats in Xochimilco.

work. They ready themselves for the spiritual sacrifices they will make during Lent. They arrange to attend mass the next day. Lent starts on the following day with the respectful celebration of Ash Wednesday.

March 21 is another national holiday in Mexico. It marks the nation-wide celebration of the birthday of Benito Juárez. Benito Juárez was a Zapotec Indian born in San Pablo Guelatao, Oaxaca. Benito became the governor of Oaxaca, and went on to become one of the most beloved presidents of Mexico.

This fiesta lasts for six days in San Pablo Guelatao. The president of Mexico and the Oaxacan governor visit the town on Benito's birthday. A civil-military celebration is held that day. The other five days are filled with folklore, food, fireworks, and dances.

Yet another holiday occurs on May 1. This is Labor Day, or Workers' Day, in Mexico. Since this is a legal holiday, almost all businesses are closed. The workers of Mexico parade in the streets of their towns, villages, and cities.

This statue of Father Miguel Hidalgo stands in the middle of a village plaza in Guadalajara. Following Mexico's Independence Day, this statue will be adorned with red, white, and green flowers to acknowledge Hidalgo's influence in the fight for a free Mexico.

One of Mexico's best-known fiestas is held on May 5. This holiday is known simply as *Cinco de Mayo*, which literally means the fifth of May. This fiesta is the celebration of Mexico's victory over the French army at Puebla in 1862.

Some residents of Puebla and Mexico City reenact the great Mexican victory at the battle of Puebla. Many Mexican cities are decorated with ribbons and flags. Military parades are held throughout the nation. Mexican school children practice with their school bands for months in advance, so that their schools may march in the Cinco de Mayo parades. Cheers of *"Viva México!"* are heard throughout the streets of the nation.

May 10 is a national holiday that has more to do with families than with history. On this day, Mexicans celebrate Mother's Day. The fiesta is particularly important since mothers are held in high regard in this culture. Mexicans honor mothers with gifts, serenades, and **mariachi** bands. To show their love and respect for their mothers many children sing the traditional song, "A Ti" (to you) to their mothers. They give their mothers candy, perfume, clothing, jewelry, or flowers. During the evening, entire families gather and **serenade** mothers.

September 16, however, is another historical

Independence Day parades in Mexico often feature colorful floats and waving flags.

fiesta. Mexican Independence Day is a more important holiday than Cinco de Mayo for most Mexicans. Independence Day commemorates the beginning of Mexico's war of independence from Spain. The celebrating begins on September 15 when crowds of people gather in the plazas or *zócalos* (town meeting places) of their hometowns. The city center in Mexico City is decorated with red, white, and green flags, flowers, and lights. Vendors sell red, white and

 The Mexican Flag contains three colors: green, white, and red. The green symbolizes independence; white symbolizes religion; and the red symbolizes union. Green, white, and red are used to decorate plazas, churches, public buildings, and homes for Mexico's Independence Day.

23

An important leader in the Mexican Independence Movement was a priest named Father Miguel Hidalgo. Hidalgo lived in Dolores, Mexico. He was planning a revolt for late fall of 1810.

The Spanish officials found out about Father Hidalgo's plans for a revolt. The Spanish government ordered the arrest of Hidalgo and his officers. The priest heard about this and rang the church bell late in the evening of September 15, 1810, to call people to the church for a mass.

When the church was full, Father Hidalgo encouraged the people to fight against the Spanish. He gave a speech that is now called the Grito de Dolores. Father Hidalgo ended his speech with the cheers "Viva México!" and "Viva la independencia!" These famous words are remembered and shouted each year on Independence Day.

green confetti, whistles, horns, papier-mâché helmets, and toys.

At 11 o'clock, crowds all across Mexico grow silent. On the last strike of the hour, the Mexican president steps out onto his palace balcony. He rings a historic bell that was used by Father Hidalgo of Dolores. He then gives the traditional speech called the *Grito de Dolores* (cry of Dolores). After his speech, the president yells, *"Viva México! Viva la independencia!"*

People all across Mexico respond by yelling the same phrases. As they do, the air fills with fireworks, confetti, streamers, and cheers. The night sky is lit up with red, white, and green.

On the following day, September 16, statues of Father Hidalgo are decorated with red, green, and white flowers. People attend rodeos, parades, bullfights, and horseback performances. In smaller villages, cockfights may be held.

Columbus Day, October 12, is another important Mexican fiesta. Mexicans refer to this day as the Day of the Races. Although it is recognized as a national holiday, most businesses and government offices remain open. Children are given the day off from school, however.

The Day of the Races acknowledges

A statue of Christopher Columbus in Mexico City. The people of Mexico celebrate October 12, the date Columbus landed in the Americas on his first voyage, as Día de la Raza (the Day of the Races). This holiday celebrates the origins of Mexico's ethnic groups.

On Mother's Day (May 10), Mexicans celebrate the sacrifices many mothers make for their children's well-being.

Columbus's role in joining the Spanish people of Europe with the native people of Mexico. This day celebrates the mixture of the Old and New Worlds more than it honors Columbus. Not surprisingly, many Mexicans have mixed feelings about Columbus; after all, the arrival of Spaniards into the world of their ancestors marked the beginning of centuries of foreign control.

After Columbus Day, come two important political holidays in November. On the first day of November, the president of Mexico gives his State of the Union Address. This coincides with the Catholic All Saints' Day. Then, on the 20th of November, Mexicans celebrate the anniversary of the Mexican Revolution of 1910. Parades, speeches, and other patriotic demonstrations commemorate the start of the war that overthrew the dictator Porfirio Díaz.

The Mexican National Holiday year ends with the celebration of Christmas on December 25. Children do not receive gifts. Instead, Mexican Catholics honor the birth of Jesus Christ on this day. Christmas is a day for Mass, reverence, family

An adobe chapel in Narayit is decorated for Christmas with lights and luminarias.

togetherness, and prayer. Although Christmas is not a political holiday, because Mexico has so many Catholics and Christians Christmas Day is recognized as a national holiday.

TEXT-DEPENDENT QUESTIONS

Why is Flag Day celebrated on February 24?

What is the name of the traditional speech given by the president of Mexico on Independence Day?

RESEARCH PROJECT

Mexicans celebrate Constitution Day on February 5, the day when the country's current constitution was passed by the legislature in 1917. A constitution is a collection of fundamental principles or guidelines that are used to govern a state. Find the Mexican constitution online (a translation of the text is available at http://www.juridicas.unam.mx/infjur/leg/constmex/pdf/consting.pdf) and read through it. What are some of the rights that the constitution promises to all Mexicans?

WORDS TO UNDERSTAND

friar—term for a member of a monastic order whose mission was to teach ordinary people.

litany—a repetitive chant.

penitents—people who are sorry for their sins.

pilgrim—a person who leaves his or her home to travel for a religious purpose, such as to visit a shrine to a particular saint.

A re-enactment of the crucifixion of Jesus is held each year on Good Friday in the village of Atotonilco. The realistic depiction draws thousands of visitors.

RELIGIOUS OBSERVANCES
PIÑATAS AND POSADAS

The religious observations of Mexico reflect the Mexican public's passionate devotion to the Catholic Church. As early as the 16th century, Spanish *friars* were sent to Mexico to convert the native people there to Catholicism. Sensing the Indians' love of ritual and ceremonies, the friars taught the native Mexicans about the Bible by using dances, plays, costumes, and masks to dramatize its stories. These practices are still evident in many religious celebrations throughout Mexico today.

Mexicans celebrate a great many religious holidays. Some of the more important ones are:

- Epiphany or Three Kings' Day, "Día de Reyes," in January
- San Antonio Abad or the Blessing of the Animals, also in January
- St. Valentine's Day in February
- Holy Week, in March or April
- "Santa Cruz" in May
- "Chalma" Lord in July
- San Francisco in October

- Virgin of Guadalupe in December
- "Las Posadas" or the Nine Days of Fiesta, which include Christmas, in December

Many of these holidays are celebrated all over Latin America.

Three Kings' Day is a traditional Catholic holiday. Mexicans exchange Christmas presents on this day. They celebrate the gifts the three wise men brought to the baby Jesus.

The children of Mexico write letters to the three magi on January fifth. They place the letters in their shoes. Next, they put nativity scenes outside their homes. They also leave hay and water for the three kings' camels. In the morning, the children awaken to find their gifts left near the nativity scenes.

Mexican bakers prepare delicious circular cakes for this day. The cakes are called the Rings of the Wise Men. A tiny porcelain doll is baked into each cake. The doll represents the baby Jesus and the gifts of the magi. The person who gets the slice of cake with the doll in it must throw another party on February 2, or Candlemas.

The story of chocolate begins in Mexico. A legend says that Quetzalcoatl, the god of light, descended upon the Toltecs of Mexico. As a gift, he gave the people the mystical cacao tree. In 1519, Spanish explorer Hernán Cortés tasted xocolatl, a chocolate drink made from the cacao bean. Cortez took the beans back to Spain. Chocolate soon became a sought-after delicacy throughout Europe.

On St. Anthony's Feast Day, a blessing of animals takes place in the Catholic churches of Mexico, since St. Anthony is the patron saint of domesticated animals. Many native Mexican cultures believed that animals had mystical powers, so this holy day was easy for the early Mexicans to accept into their culture.

The Catedral Metropolitana de la Asunción de María in Mexico City is decorated for Christmas.

Pets and livestock are decorated with flowers, colored streamers, and ribbons for St. Anthony's Day. Many people parade their chickens, horses, dogs, cats, and other animals around their towns. The animals are taken to church and blessed by a Catholic priest.

On St. Valentine's Day, Mexicans acknowledge the importance of love and friendship in their lives. Balloon vendors sell colorful, heart-shaped declarations of love in the streets. Chocolates and cards are sold in the stores and street markets. Young men stay up late into the night serenading their girlfriends.

Holy Week, the week before Easter Sunday, is time of prayer all over Mexico. Taxco hosts a world-famous religious festival between Palm Sunday and Easter. Thousands of *pilgrims* and *penitents* participate in the reenactments of the crucifixion of Christ.

Many towns prepare all year long for this week. They stage grand reenactments of Christ's Last Supper, Betrayal, and Judgment; the Procession of the 12 Stations of the Cross; the Crucifixion; and finally, the Resurrection. On

Mexicans participate in a Holy Week procession in San Miguel de Allende. Holy Week is a time of solemn observance for Mexican Christians.

Good Friday and Easter Sunday, churches are filled with those attending mass. Flower decorations and palm crosses can be found everywhere. Each community celebrates the holiday in its own way, but one tradition that is popular throughout the whole country is the breaking of *cascarones* (colored eggshells filled with confetti) over the heads of friends and family.

The Saturday before Easter, Mexicans participate in a ritual called "The Burning of Judas." (Judas was the apostle who is said to have betrayed Jesus Christ.) Mexicans burn cardboard likenesses of Judas. Some use this night to protest social and political problems by burning likenesses of people they consider to be modern-day bad guys or "Judases." Sometimes the Judas images are stuffed full of fireworks. This way, they not only burn; they blow up!

On Easter Sunday, Catholics attend Mass and take Holy Communion in honor of the resurrection of Jesus Christ. Festive crowds gather in every town plaza after these church services. Street vendors sell food, balloons, and toys. Children and adults get ready to return to school and work, as this day signals the end of their two-week vacations.

Mexican Catholics have a deep love for the mother of Jesus Christ, whom they call Our Lady of Guadalupe. December 12 is the day she is said to have appeared as an Aztec princess to Juan Diego in 1591. Pilgrimages to

On May 3, Holy Cross Day, Mexicans honor masons. The tradition began at the start of the Spanish colonial period in Mexico, when the churches were still being built. On Holy Cross Day, the priests would ask the masons to make crosses to place on the churches' highest peaks. The masons would climb atop the churches to secure the crosses there.

The bosses of Mexican masons still honor them on this day by letting them take long lunches. Some bosses even bring their masons food and beer. Masons and their families often have a special dinner at home to celebrate this day.

After the Lady of Guadalupe, an Aztec embodiment of the Virgin Mary, spoke to Juan Diego in the Aztec language, Diego told the local bishop that the Virgin had requested that a church be built on Tepeyac Hill outside Mexico City. The bishop did not believe him. He asked Juan Diego to provide him with some sort of proof.

The Lady of Guadalupe appeared again and told Juan to gather roses that had suddenly appeared on the snow-covered ground. He gathered the roses, and wrapped them inside his mantle. Then Juan Diego brought the roses to the bishop.

The bishop was amazed. Not only had Juan Diego brought him roses in the winter, but on Juan Diego's mantle was an image of the Virgin! The bishop now believed that Juan's visions were real. The Virgin appeared to Juan Diego two more times. In 1593 Bishop Zumárraga had the church built that Juan Diego had requested for the Virgin Mary. The mantle was enshrined in the church. In 1754 Pope Benedict XIV issued a decree dedicating December 12th Masses to "Our Lady of Guadalupe." Our Lady of Guadalupe was designated Patroness of Latin America in 1910. Pope Pius XII declared her to be the Patroness of the Americas in 1945.

the Basilica of Our Lady of Guadalupe in Mexico City, processions in cities all over the country, dance performances, and special masses all mark the celebrations on December 12.

Because the story says that Our Lady of Guadalupe spoke in the Aztec language to an Aztec man, she is particularly beloved by the Mexican people. On her special day, people bring roses to her church. The Catholics of Mexico, who make up about 90 percent of the total population, all honor her on this day.

Christmas in Mexico is also an important holiday season with deep-seated traditions. *Posada* is a vital part of this celebration. It honors Mary and Joseph's cold and difficult journey from Nazareth to Bethlehem in search of shelter. Every night from December 16 through Christmas Eve, a get-together is held in someone's home. The people eat, drink, and

Catholic pilgrims visit the basilica of Our Lady of Guadalupe in Mexico City on December 12.

enjoy each other's company. The children enjoy special candies and fruits. At twilight, all of the party guests gather outside the house.

A small child is chosen to be dressed as an angel and lead the procession. Other children, carrying images of Mary and Joseph, follow this angel. Following

During Posada celebrations, star-shaped piñatas are used to represent the star that shone over the place where Jesus was born.

them are still more children dressed in special robes and costumes. Finally, at the end of the procession, are the adults and musicians.

Everyone sings and carries lit candles. They parade around their neighborhood streets, and then they stop at a chosen house to sing a traditional **litany**. In the song, Mary and Joseph request shelter for the night. The song ends when those waiting behind the closed door turn the procession away. The group then parades ahead to a second home where the scene is repeated. At the third stop, the pilgrims are told that there is no room in the *posada* (inn), but they are welcome to sleep in the stable. Now, the doors of the house are pushed open, and the beggars are welcomed inside.

After the religious processions, come fireworks, dancing, drinking, and singing. The children are given a piñata to break at the end of this evening. Posada piñatas are traditionally made in the shape of a star to remember the light that brought the three kings to the newborn Jesus.

When the Posada is about to end, every guest receives a small gift, or *aguinaldo*, which is usually a package containing cookies, dried and fresh fruit, and *colación* (assorted candies). On Christmas Eve, Posada ends with midnight mass at the village church.

After mass, the village begins their celebration of the birth of Jesus Christ. One very old Christmas tradition is for all of the Christians in the village to gather in front of a *nacimiento* (nativity scene) to sing *villancicos* (Christmas carols) to the newborn Christ child.

Christmas day is a day for church and quiet reflection in Mexico, a day for rest and family togetherness. Christmas is the last major religious holiday of the year.

TEXT-DEPENDENT QUESTIONS

What is the feast day for Our Lady of Guadalupe?

What group of workers are honored on Holy Cross Day?

RESEARCH PROJECT

Although the Mexican government does not recognize an official state religion, more than 80 percent of Mexicans are Roman Catholic, while another 11 percent are members of other Christian denominations. Do some research and write a paper explaining what historical events caused Mexico to be predominantly Catholic/Christian today.

WORDS TO UNDERSTAND

equinox—one of the two times during the year when day and night are equal in length.

molé—a spicy sauce made out of chilies and chocolate and usually served with meat.

mummers—people who go merrymaking in disguises.

pagan—someone who follows a religion with more than one god.

pre-Columbian—before the arrival of Columbus in America.

tamales—ground meat seasoned with chili, rolled in cornmeal dough, wrapped in cornhusks, and steamed.

tequila—a liquor made from the sap of a Mexican plant.

Musicians perform in a cemetery in Aguacalientes during the Day of the Dead. This festival, observed on November 2, celebrates the souls of friends and family members who have passed away.

ANCIENT FESTIVALS
FLYING MEN AND SUGAR SKULLS

Festivals and holidays have been celebrated since ancient times. The earliest festivals were connected with offerings to the gods; some were also remembrances for the dead. Planting time and harvest time were other occasions for special ritual celebrations. Candlemas, Corpus Christi, and the Day of the Dead are three holidays whose roots and traditions go back to the Aztecs of *pre-Columbian* Mexico.

February 2 is Candlemas, the end of the Christmas season for most modern Mexicans. In today's Mexico, cities and towns revel and make merry on this day with parties, parades, and bullfights. The streets are decorated with lanterns. Whoever found a doll in the cake on Three Kings' Day must host a big Candlemas party. The holiday celebrates both the Day of the Blessing of the seeds or crops and the Catholic celebration of the day Mary took the baby Jesus to the temple. In Mexico's smaller towns and villages, paper dolls of *brujas* (witches) are placed in the fields and gardens, while many Mexicans also attend mass on this day, mixing superstition and religion. The brown brujas are believed to ward off evil spirits, and white brujas are said to attract good spirits.

In late March, the Return of the Sun Serpent (the spring *equinox*) is celebrated at Chichen Itza in the Yucatán Peninsula. Local residents host a large fiesta that features light and sound shows, music, and dancing. Thousands of Mexicans and tourists come here to watch for the afternoon shadow of the snake-god Kukulkán. The people watch as the sun lights up the layers of the El Castillo Pyramid, forming sunlit triangles on one side of El Castillo from the top to the bottom. As the sun rises in the sky, more and more triangles appear down the side of the pyramid. Eventually, the sunlight shines upon a large snake's head at the bottom of the pyramid. This snake is Kukulkán, the Mayan god known as the Feathered Serpent. The Maya believed Kukulkán traveled down from the heavens to carry wealth and good fortune.

Mexican Catholics celebrate the religious festival of Corpus Christi, or the body of Christ, 60 days after Easter Sunday. Like much of the Mexican population, this holiday has become *mestizo*; in other words, it is a mix of Native American and Spanish. On Corpus Christi, Mexicans honor the religious holiday as well as a native tradition celebrating the first fruits of summer.

At this time of year, the dance of *Los Voladores* (the Flying Men) is most likely to take place all over Mexico. This dance is a 1,500-year-old rite originally started by the Totonac people. The dance is believed to have begun at El Tejín, near Papantla, Mexico. It spread throughout Mexico and into parts of Guatemala. A special square

The Aztecs planned their festivals over an 18-month year. Each month contained 20 days. This left the Aztecs with an extra five days that did not fit into any of their months. These extra five days were thought to be very dangerous days when evil spirits could do great harm to the people. The people generally did as little as possible during this time, preferring to hide from the evil spirits.

Each year, thousands of tourists gather at the ancient pyramid in Chichen Itza to celebrate the spring equinox, just as the Mayans did.

was even reserved for it in Tenochtitlán, the Aztec capital. Today, the dance is performed all over Mexico for tourists, but the Papantla Totonac Voladores are still known as the best in the country.

Five men dressed in multicolored outfits perform the *Voladore* ceremony atop a wooden pole that's as high as 105 feet. Sometimes, the men wear costumes to make themselves look like brightly colored birds. Four of the men perch on a tiny platform, wrapping their legs with long ropes, which are attached to the

Voladores (flyers) hang suspended from ropes. These men perform a pre-Columbian ritual that was intended to bring rain for crops. They jump head-first from a tall pole attached to a wound-up rope, which unwinds as they spin and fall to the ground.

pole. The four men are thought to represent the north, south, east, and west—or perhaps earth, wind, fire, and water. The fifth man dances at the center of the pole on a tiny platform, playing a reed flute and a small drum as he dances. The four men then fall backward into the air, swinging around the pole. Hanging upside down with arms out-stretched, they twirl back toward the ground. Each flyer circles the pole 13 times during his fall. Between the four, this makes a total of 52 revolutions, one for each week of the year. They stop just inches from the ground, then flip and land on their feet.

But Mexico's most famous fiesta, outside of Cinco de Mayo, falls on November 1 and 2. November 1 is All Saints' Day, and the Day of the Dead is November 2. Although each day has religious significance for the Catholic Church, the Mexican celebrations are really throwbacks to pre-Columbian rituals.

The original rites of the Day of the Dead have been traced back to the festivities held during the Aztec month of Miccailhuitontli. The Aztecs offered these celebrations in honor of children and the dead. They held their celebrations in the summer, however.

Spanish friars and priests considered the Aztec festival to be *pagan* and sinful. The Catholics wanted to change the celebration. By moving the date of the Day of the Dead festivities, they were trying to Christianize them. The Spanish Catholics hoped that the Aztecs would replace their Day of the Dead practices with the Catholic rituals for All Saints' and All Souls' Days. Because of the priests' efforts, Mexicans now celebrate the

The Aztecs worshiped the corn and rain gods from February through March. Poles were erected and decorated with banners in their homes and temples. Children were carried into the mountains and sacrificed to the rain gods. Quetzalcoatl, the greatest of the Aztec gods, was asked to use his powers as a god of the wind to push the rains away.

Day of the Dead in November, instead of in the summer. The celebration has retained most of its Aztec flavor, however. It is a fiesta dedicated to the dead, a time to remember lost loved ones, but the fiesta is not a somber time. Instead, it is a celebration of life, as well as a time of homage to the dead.

Skull-shaped candies are sold in the streets. *Ofrendas*, or little shrines covered with offerings, are built to honor departed family members. Some Mexicans build altars that look like they belong in a Catholic church, while other Mexicans build the traditional native-type altars used by their ancestors. These altars are pyramid shaped with five levels. Each level represents a stage in the life cycle. The first level is birth. Life and death are the second and third stages. The fourth level represents the evolution and cleansing of the soul. The fifth and final level symbolizes a return to new life.

Yellow marigolds, or *cempazúchitls*, are placed on the shrines, as these were the Aztecs' flower for the dead. Skeleton-shaped decorations hang in the windows of most homes and shops. Cemeteries are crowded with families, who clean and decorate the final resting places of their loved ones. Marigolds are also used to form paths to the altars. These paths are believed to guide the smallest dead back home. These small dead are the departed children of Mexican families. On altars for these *angelitos* (little angels), candies, milk, sweet **tamales**, and the traditional *pan de muertos* (bread of the dead) will be placed. The *angelitos* are thought to return before the other dead, on October 30 or 31. The families welcome the dead children with toys and other gifts. The *angelitos* then leave before the arrival of the other dead.

The altars for the adult dead, or the faithful dead as they are called, are made ready by the first of November. They are laden with offerings such as **tequila**, tamales, **molé**, fruit, and *pan de muertos*. *Pan de muertos* is often

Figures of skeletons on a carnival float in Aguacalientes. Celebrations for the Day of the Dead may appear morbid to outsiders, but they carry a great deal of significance for Mexican participants.

formed into the shape of an oval, as many once believed that the spirit or soul is oval shaped. People also leave bread and water in corners of the local churches for those dead who have no remaining family to care for them. The graveyards are decorated with wreaths of orange and purple flowers. Bells ring

The Day of the Dead altar features sugar skulls, candles, and flowers.

in the arrival of the faithful dead. Candles are lit to guide the faithful dead back to their relatives' homes. A candle is lit for each lost soul, and the cemetery glows with the flames of hundreds of candles. Late into the evening, women pray for the dead, while the men sing and drink.

On the Day of the Dead, masked comedians, called *comparsas*, travel from home to home. Other actors and musicians often accompany them. Together, they make fun of the living.

On November 2, a special family feast is prepared. Again, *pan de muertos* is served. Like the doll in the bread for Three Kings' Day, a toy skeleton is often hidden in these loaves of bread. It is good luck to find the skeleton.

On the evening of November 2, people called **mummers** run around the town with masks on their faces. The mummers look for stubborn souls who refuse to return to the land of the dead. The mummers' job is to make sure that the stubborn souls go back where they belong.

After the mummers have chased away the stubborn dead, families begin to clean up. The altars are taken down. The skeleton decorations are put away. Life goes back to normal; the Day of the Dead is over until next year. The new year will bring a new cycle of ancient fiestas and celebrations.

TEXT-DEPENDENT QUESTIONS

What flower is traditionally placed on shrines for the Day of the Dead? Why?

At what time of year do the Voladores typically perform in Mexico?

RESEARCH PROJECT

Using the Internet, find out about Kukulkán, the Mayan serpent-deity whose temple is found in Chichen Itza. Share stories and folklore about this deity with your class.

 WORDS TO UNDERSTAND

guava—a pear-shaped, sweet fruit that is typically yellow or pink.

indigenous—native to a particular region.

mescal—a liquor from a Mexican cactus.

salsa—Latin-American music containing elements of rhythm and blues, jazz, and rock music.

Mexican weddings are a joyful affair, not only for the couple but also for the families and surrounding community. Traditionally, celebrations include Mexican food, music, and dancing.

LOCAL FESTIVALS
PERSONAL PARTIES, FOOD FIESTAS, AND FERIAS

E very village and almost every neighborhood of Mexico's larger towns and cities has a preferred saint (or patron) in whose honor local festivals are held once a year. These patron fiestas are often *novenarios*—nine-day celebrations. Patron saint *novenarios* are celebrated differently from place to place.

Personal parties include weddings, baptisms, First Communions, and Confirmation celebrations. Wedding anniversaries are also cause for large personal fiestas. Births and birthdays are celebrated as well.

In Mexico, the 15th birthday of a Catholic young woman is called her *Quinceañera*, a very special celebration in her life. She will attend a church service dressed in a fancy dress with five to seven maids of honor to attend her, just as a bride would have. She also has five to seven chambermaids.

The young woman's parents and godparents sit with her during the church service. The mass celebrates the fact that she has reached sexual maturity and is now of marriageable age. Often the masses will feature a long sermon on

A girl is blindfolded as she prepares to takes her turn at trying to break the piñata at a birthday party. The papier-mâché creations are hung from a string and usually contain candy and small toys.

how a young woman of this age should behave.

After the mass, the chambermaids and maids of honor pass out small gifts called *bolos* to the guests. While the bolos are being passed out, the young woman takes her bouquet and offers it up to the Virgin Mary. Often, she will put her flowers at the feet of a statue of the Virgin of Guadalupe.

Next, there is a party for the young woman. If she chooses not to have a party, she is also allowed to go on a trip instead, but most young women prefer to have a party. To reduce the financial burden, her parents ask her godparents and other friends to help sponsor this event.

The party will have plenty food and music. **Salsa** and mariachi tunes encourage lively dancing. However, the most important dance is a traditional waltz. The

A traditional mariachi band fills a Mexican plaza with music. Mariachi bands are hired to play their cheerful music at restaurants and tourist spots, as well as festivals.

festejada (celebrant) and her favorite *chambelán* (escort) dance together to this song as the other partygoers look on. Then comes the customary toast. The festejada must also cut her birthday cake. The cake is made up of many layers and decorated to match the young woman's dress.

The celebration is a very important moment in the young woman's life. She is now allowed to date, and she is now eligible to marry.

Mexico also hosts a variety of food festivals and *ferias* (fairs) each year. A feria celebrates the local harvest. The food that is important to that area is featured and honored with samples of farmers' best wares. Dances, carnival rides, bullfights, fireworks, and food stalls add to the excitement.

Canelas, a city in Durango, hosts a coffee and **guava** fair from February 23 to February 26 of each year. Those who attend this food fair can try different

A Mexican family celebrates a young girl's 15th birthday. This special day is called a Quinceañera, and marks the symbolic departure of a girl from adolescence to womanhood.

kinds of local coffees. Guava juices, marmalades, and preserves are available to sample and purchase.

On March 11, the village of Dzula, a small *indigenous* village in Quintana Roo, puts on a traditional Mayan food fiesta. Their festival focuses on the foods of their ancestors, the Maya of the Yucatán Peninsula.

April is the month for Mexico's largest food fair, the Wine Festival in Aguascalientes. This festival lasts for half a month! There are many events to attend, including bullfights and cockfights.

Another food festival that lasts half a month is the Rice Festival in Escárcega, Campeche. It lasts from May 15 until May 31. Seafood and rice dishes are the main fare for this festival.

June 18 is the starting date for the famous Vanilla Festival in Papantla, Veracruz. Booths sell local food and beverage specialties. The flying *voladores* perform. The artisans sell small animal images and baskets woven from vanilla bean pods. Sachets and vanilla perfumes are also for sale. Paplanta is one of the world's largest vanilla producers.

From July 17 to 23 the Oaxaca Mescal Festival takes place. The people of Oaxaca build special wooden houses to display various blends of **mescal**. The Oaxacans are an artistic people, and they sell many arts and crafts at this fair, too.

August is the time for the Corn Festival in Tala, Nayarit. This celebration probably dates back to the ancient Aztecs and their corn celebrations. Besides a great variety of corn dishes, the fiesta offers cockfights, bullfights, and dances.

September 14 to 16 are the dates for the Peach Fair in Surutato, Sinaloa. Peach juice, preserves, and deserts are featured at this festival. Like at other festivals, the streets are filled with folk dancing and music.

On October 14 through 17, the Bread Fair takes place in Cholula, Puebla. The village constructs a giant brick oven in the town square. Bakers from the town of Cholula and other nearby villages and towns take turns demonstrating their skills at

 One baptism tradition that is practiced among some of Mexico's indigenous peoples is the placing of tiny farm hoes in the hands of the male children. The female children have small spindles for weaving cotton or wool placed in their hands. This is to honor the traditional roles as farmers and weavers that they will take on when they grow up.

53

A vendor dishes out fajitas for hungry customers at a small food festival. Along with its music and customs, traditional cuisine helps to keep the Mexican culture thriving.

traditional Mexican bread baking.

On December 23, the people of the town of Oaxaca hold their radish festival. The radishes of Oaxaca grow to extraordinary lengths and often take very interesting shapes. Beautiful sculptures are made out of them, and a contest is held for the best radish sculpture. Entire nativity scenes are carved out of radishes! The people then have a parade with floats and music on Christmas Eve.

New Year's Eve marks the beginning of a fresh round of fiestas and festivals. The celebrations begin anew. Many visitors travel to Mexico just to witness one of these many fiestas.

55

TEXT-DEPENDENT QUESTIONS
What is the name of the traditional music often played at Mexican fiestas?
How long does the typical *novenario* last?

RESEARCH PROJECT
The Quinceañera, or 15th birthday celebration for young women, is observed by people of Hispanic descent in the United States, as well as in other Latin American countries. Using the Internet, find out details of the Quinceañera celebration in some countries other than Mexico. What are the differences? What are some elements of this fiesta that are the same in all countries?

SERIES GLOSSARY

Adobe   A building material made of mud and straw.

Amerindian A term for the indigenous peoples of North and South America before the arrival of Europeans in the late 15th century.

Conquistador Any one of the Spanish leaders of the conquest of the Americas in the 1500s.

Criollo   A resident of New Spain who was born in North America to parents of Spanish ancestry. In the social order of New Spain, criollos ranked above mestizos.

Fiesta   A Mexican party or celebration.

Haciendas Large Mexican ranches.

Maquiladoras Factories created to attract foreign business to Mexico by allowing them to do business cheaply.

Mariachi   A Mexican street band that performs a distinctive type of music utilizing guitars, violins, and trumpets.

Mesoamerica The region of southern North America that was inhabited before the arrival of the Spaniards.

Mestizo   A person of mixed Amerindian and European (typically Spanish) descent.

Nahuatl   The ancient language spoken by the Aztecs; still spoken by many modern Mexicans.

New Spain Name for the Spanish colony that included modern-day Mexico. This vast area of North America was conquered by Spain in the 1500s and ruled by the Spanish until 1821.

Plazas   The central open squares at the center of Spanish cities.

Pre-Columbian Referring to a time before the 1490s, when Christopher Columbus landed in the Americas.

56

An Independence Day celebration in Chiapas.

A Maya ceremony combining both elements of traditional culture and Catholicism is performed in Palenque, Chiapas.

FURTHER READING

Chávez, Alicia Hernández. *Mexico: A Brief History*. Berkeley: University of California Press, 2006.

Coe, Michael D., and Rex Koontz. *Mexico: From the Olmecs to the Aztecs*. New York: Thames and Hudson, 2008.

Gritzner, Charles F. *Mexico*. New York: Chelsea House, 2012.

Hamnet, Brian R. *A Concise History of Mexico*. New York: Cambridge University Press, 2006.

Kent, Deborah. *Mexico*. New York: Children's Press, 2012.

Mayor, Guy. *Mexico: A Quick Guide to Customs and Etiquette*. New York: Kuperard, 2006.

Meyer, Michael C., et al. *The Course of Mexican History*. New York: Oxford University Press, 2002.

Santibanez, Roberto, with J.J. Goode. *Tacos, Tortas, and Tamales: Flavors from the Griddles, Pots, and Streetside Kitchens of Mexico*. New York: Houghton Mifflin, 2014.

Sterling, David. *Yucatán: Recipes from a Culinary Expedition*. Austin: University of Texas Press, 2014.

Torpie, Kate. *Cinco de Mayo*. New York: Crabtree, 2008.

Vijnanananda, Swami. *The Myths of Mexico and Peru*. Charleston, S.C.: BiblioBazaar, 2008.

INTERNET RESOURCES

Mesoweb
http://www.mesoweb.com/welcome.html#externalresources

National Geographic
http://kids.nationalgeographic.com/kids/places/find/mexico

CIA World Factbook
https://www.cia.gov/library/publications/the-world-factbook/geos/mx.html

History of Mexico
http://www.history.com/topics/mexico

Mexico Connect
http://www.mexconnect.com

Mexico Online
http://www.mexonline.com/history.htm

INDEX

63

PICTURE CREDITS

Page
2:    IMS Communications, Ltd.
3:    used under license from
      Shutterstock, Inc.
7:    Chad Zuber/Shutterstock
11:   Tipograffias/Shutterstock
12:   Richard Thornton/Shutterstock
15:   Stanislaw Tokarski/Shutterstock
16:   Corbis Images
18:   Tipograffias/Shutterstock
21:   Gary Yim/Shutterstock
22:   Bill Perry/Shutterstock
23:   Tipograffias/Shutterstock
25:   Jess Kraft/Shutterstock
26:   Snapshot Photos
27:   Sumikophoto/Shutterstock
28:   used under license from
      Shutterstock, Inc.
31:   Stefano Ember/Shutterstock

32:   used under license from
      Shutterstock, Inc.
35:   Chad Zuber/Shutterstock
36:   Fer Gregory/Shutterstock
38:   Sunsinger/Shutterstock
41:   Borna Mirahmadian/Shutterstock
42:   Ilya Frankazoid/Shutterstock
45:   Sunsinger/Shutterstock
46:   AG Cuesta/Shutterstock
48:   used under license from
      Shutterstock, Inc.
50:   Blend Images
51:   IMS Communications, Ltd.
52:   Blend Images
54:   IMS Communications, Ltd.
57:   Jorge R. Gonzalez/Shutterstock
58:   Chad Zuber/Shutterstock
61:   Tipograffias/Shutterstock

ABOUT THE AUTHOR

Colleen Madonna Flood Williams resides in Soldotna, Alaska, with her husband, Paul R. Williams, and son Dillon Meehan. She is the author of an art unit for elementary students, entitled THE ANXIOUS ART TEACHER. She has been published in a variety of online and print publications. She is also the author of *The Geography of Mexico*, and *The People of Mexico*.